HOLD YOUR HORSES!
ANIMAL ENCYCLOPEDIA
HORSES FOR KIDS
CHILDREN'S BIOLOGICAL SCIENCE OF HORSES BOOKS

BOBO's
LITTLE BRIANIAC BOOKS
educational & informative books for children
(PRE-K / K-12)

Kids, you are invited to read and find amazing facts about horses.

The horse was believed to have evolved 45 to 55 million years. It was believed to have originated from a small multi-toed creature.

Through the passing of times, horses transformed into a large and single-toed animal.

These friendly animals were believed to have been domesticated by humans between 4000 and 3000 BC.

They are
noted for their
remarkable
speed and
fantastic balance
which they use
in escaping from
their predators
in the wild.

Horses come in over 350 different breeds and ponies. The last working animals to be domesticated are the horses.

We call the male horse as stallion while the female horse is called a mare. Filly is the name of a young female horse and colt is the name of young male horse.

A baby horse is called a foal. Sire is the name of the father horse and dam is the name of the mother horse. Pony is the term used for a fully grown small horse.

A mare gets pregnant for 11 months and gives birth to a single foal or twins. Foals are usually born at night under darkness and away from danger.

Horses may come in different colors but the most common colors are brown, black, chestnut, cream, grey, dun, bay and palomino.

Arabian horse
is known to be
the most popular
horse breed
in the world.

Horses have an average life span of 25 years. Some may reach 30 years.

Horses don't pant like dogs. It is because horses can't breathe through their mouth.

Horses have four natural paces namely, trot, gallop, walk and canter. These animals have good memory for they can remember you if you've been with them for a long time.

Working and travelling horses have their hooves protected by metal shoes. A farrier or blacksmith is the person who takes care of the horse's feet.

Horses have the biggest eyes among the earth land animals.

Read more interesting facts about this solid-hoofed plant eating four legged animal and learn to appreciate its worth.

Made in the USA
Lexington, KY
22 April 2019